Building a l from "*I Can't*" to "*I DID!*"

Creating Independent Learners Through Culturally Responsive Teaching

Jenn Kleiber

Book Study

Published by Self Publish -N- 30 Days

Copyright 2019 Jenn Kleiber.

All rights reserved worldwide. No part of this book may be reproduced or transmitted in any form or by any means electronic or mechanical, including photocopying, recording or by any information storage and retrieval system without written permission from Jenn Kleiber.

Printed in the United States of America

ISBN: 978-1-70650-769-7 1. Non-fiction 2. Education 3. Cultural Competence

Jenn Kleiber Building a Bridge from "I Can't" to "I DID!" Book Study

Disclaimer/Warning:
This book is intended for lecture and informative purposes only. The author or publisher does not guarantee that anyone following these steps will be successful in education or teaching. The author and publisher shall have neither liability or responsibility to anyone with respect to any loss or damage caused, or alleged to be caused, directly or indirectly by the information contained in this book.

All material used in the workbook with rights belonging to another author or organization is cited in the related book, Building a Bridge from "I Can't" to "I DID!".

Table of Contents

Introduction and Chapter 1: The WHAT and WHY of Culture 1

Chapter 2: Learn or Protect: The Survival Mode Struggle 11

Chapter 3: Teaching by Reaching All Students 17

Chapter 4: Facing and Moving Past the Unique Challenges of Students of Poverty 25

Part III and Chapter 5: The Power of an Alliance 29

Chapter 6: The Beauty of a Culturally Rich Environment 35

Chapter 7: The Effectiveness of Hitting the Learning Target 41

APPENDIX

Cultural Survey 49

Cultural Survey — Students 51

VOICE CHART 53

Culturally Responsive Teaching Checklist 55

Introduction and Chapter 1

The WHAT and WHY of Culture

1. Discuss the quotes below found at the end of the Introduction and the beginning of Chapter 1. What do these quotes mean to you? What is inspiring about these quotes? What is difficult?

> *"Every child deserves a champion: an adult who will never give up on them, who understands the power of connection and insists they become the best they can possibly be."*
> — Rita Pierson

The WHAT and WHY of Culture

> *"The best thing about being a teacher is that it matters. The hardest thing about being a teacher is that it matters every day."*
>
> — **Todd Whitaker**

_____
_____
_____
_____
_____
_____
_____
_____

2. Are you prepared to be self-reflective? How do you think this ongoing practice will help you as you grow as a culturally responsive teacher?

_____
_____
_____
_____
_____
_____
_____
_____
_____
_____
_____

3. Think about the four ideas that culture defines for students on page 8.

- What they will focus their attention on,
- How they interpret the world and give it meaning,
- What background knowledge they bring to learning, and
- How they will value that learning.

After reading these sections, how would you say that culture defines each of these points for you specifically in your learning process?

4 The WHAT and WHY of Culture

4. Think about the students you have the privilege to teach. How is your cultural lens different from theirs? How is it similar?

5. What are some elements of your surface culture? (food, traditions, clothes, etc.)

6. Where does your deep culture lean the most heavily—individualist or collectivist? Give specific examples.

7. Do you facilitate your class primarily from an individualist of collectivist perspective? Think deeply! What are your expectations—grades? Completion of tasks? Interaction?

8. Thinking of Question #6, what parts of your class or instruction facilitate student success consistently? Why do you think this is? What areas may need to be tweaked?

9. Discuss scenarios on Pages 19–21. Remember that "the **collectivist culture** tends to emphasize the needs and goals of the group as a whole over the needs and desires of the individual", and "the **individualistic culture** emphasizes the individual over the group." (p. 18). How would you handle each of these scenarios?

Chapter 2

Learn or Protect: The Survival Mode Struggle

1. Read the quote from Chapter 2. Do you agree with this quote? Why or why not?

"Our children are only as brilliant as we allow them to be."
— Eric Micha'el Leventhal

_____
_____
_____
_____
_____

2. How does it make you *feel* when you read that African American and Latino students historically and currently are scoring an average of 2 grade levels behind their white counterparts (nationwide)?

3. Read this quote from Zaretta Hammond.

> *"As educators, we have to recognize that we help maintain the achievement gap when we don't teach advance cognitive skills to students we label as "disadvantaged" because of their language, gender, race, or socio-economic status. Many children start school with the small learning gaps, but as they progress through school, the gap between African American and Latino and White students grows because we don't teach them how to be independent learners." (2015)*

Do you agree with this? Does it have to be this way? What are your thoughts as you read this quote?

_____
_____
_____
_____
_____
_____
_____
_____
_____
_____
_____
_____
_____
_____
_____
_____
_____
_____
_____
_____

4. What are some of the "threats" that may be getting sent to many of your students' amygdalae? Are there any "threats" that you can control?

5. Think about some of your most unsuccessful students. Can you determine their primary response to threat—fight, flight, freeze or appease? What does this behavior look like in your classroom?

10. Are there any additional scenarios that you deal with in your class that could have a different outcome based on if you handle it through the lens of collectivism or individualism?

Strategies for Classroom Implementation

BUILDING BACKGROUND
To Build Previous Knowledge

- **Novel Ideas**: In Novel Ideas, students are broken into groups of 5 or 6. Teacher gives the class a concept (for example, *fraction*), and students are given one minute to independently make a list of anything that is related or reminds them of the concept. After the minute has passed, the teacher calls time. One person in each group starts and calls out one word off of his or her list. If the other students have it on their list, they check it off. If they don't, they add it to the bottom. Then the next person calls out a word. This process repeats until every word has been called off of every list. Once all words have been called off of a student's list, the student says, "pass." Once everyone has "passed," that group is done. When the group is done, each person in the group will have the same checklist.

- **Knowledge Checklist**: This strategy can be used as a self-assessment tool and as a way to activate previous knowledge. Students are given a list of concepts or vocabulary terms that they will learn in the upcoming instruction. Students are self-assessing themselves on a continuum of "Could teach it," "Know it pretty well," "Am familiar with it", "Don't know it very well", and "Never heard of it." As the concept is introduced in the lesson, they can refer back to their knowledge checklist and move the checkmark along the continuum.

- ****Suggestion**: If you have students who feel like they can teach it, make sure they can teach it to you first, and if they are on track, give them the opportunity to teach it to the class!

- **Anticipation Guide**: An anticipation guide can be used in two different ways. First, it can be used to gauge students' prior experiences (we will discuss this in the next box). Second, it can be used to pre-assess and activate previous knowledge. Students are given an anticipation guide with agree/disagree statements from the content. Students are to answer agree or disagree to each statement. After teaching the lesson, students can revisit the anticipation guide to see if they still agree with the answers they first wrote down.

- **Realia/Visuals**: Showing students an actual item (realia) or visuals, such as photographs, pictures, videos, charts, etc. can activate previous knowledge.

Prior Experiences

- **Anticipation Guide**: An Anticipation Guide can be used to build on prior experiences by asking agree/disagree questions based on the students' opinions or experiences prior to starting a new concept.

- **Quick Write**: A Quick Write can be used in many ways. One of the best ways is to use a Quick Write to build on prior experiences. Again, asking prompts that require students to give their opinion or thoughts on a situation can connect their experiences to new learning.

- **Free Association**: In Free Association, the teacher puts a word up on the board or chart paper. Students call out words or phrases that are relevant or that remind them of the concept. This allows students to build off of each other's knowledge and experiences as well.

Build Vocabulary

- **Word Wall**: This strategy simply gets the words that are currently being learned up on the wall in a clear manner.

- **Musical Words**: Musical Words is a strategy that combines music, movement, and vocabulary! In this strategy, the teacher will break the students in groups of no more than five and have the students sit in a circle. Each student will be numbered (1, 2, 3, 4, 5). Each student chooses a word off of the word wall and writes it on a post-it note (make sure that each student in the group has the same size and color of post it notes) and turns it face down. When the music starts, students pass their words (still face down) to the right. When the music stops, the teacher calls out a number, and that numbered student holds the word they have up to their forehead without looking at it. The rest of the group gives clues to the student so that the student can guess their word. Once they guess it, the next number will hold their word up, and this will continue going until the teacher begins playing the music again. I would suggest doing 3–4 rounds. (EL Saber, 2015)

- **Draw Me**: Students will be paired with a partner. They need one piece of paper and one pencil between them. Partner A will start as the illustrator, and Partner B will be the guesser. Partner A begins drawing a word on the word wall as Partner B tries to guess the word. As soon as Partner B guesses the word, Partner A chooses another word and begins illustrating. Partner A is the illustrator for a minute. When the timer goes off, the partners switch, and Partner B becomes the illustrator and Partner A becomes the guesser. (EL Saber, 2015)

- **Concept Definition Map**: In a concept definition map, the idea is that students make personal connections to prior knowledge and experience, as they go deeper with a new concept. They may answer sentence frames like, "This reminds me of…" "An example is…" "A non-example is…" "An illustration is…" "An analogy is…" Typically this is done in a graphic organizer, such as a web. (EL Saber, 2015)

6. Go through each section on pages 36–37 on how to lower the affective filter.

- Create a Positive Environment
- Provide Appropriate Supports and Scaffolds
- Provide Relevant Tasks
- Provide Clear Directions
- Provide Order

How do you intentionally lower the affective filter in your students? Which of these do you do naturally? Where could you be more intentional?

7. Do you have students who are struggling with learned helplessness or on that path?

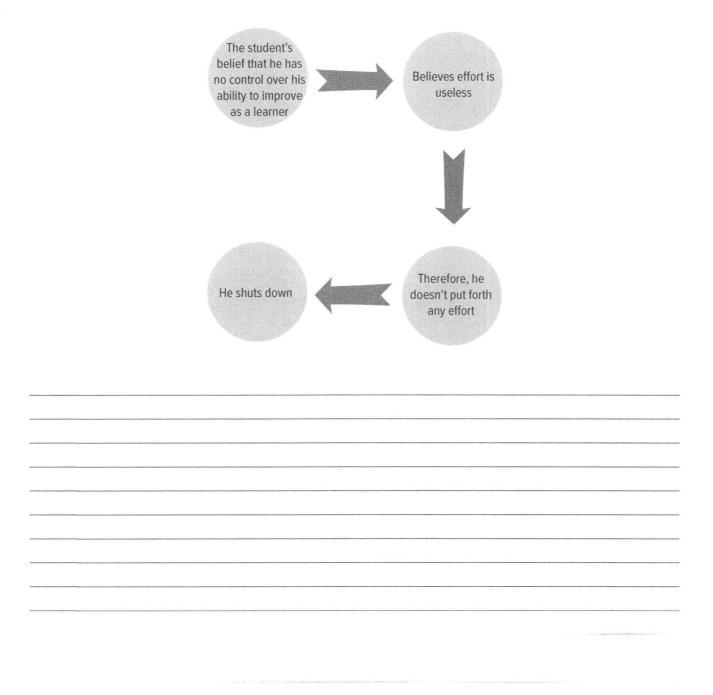

8. In your grade and content area, what concepts fall under locale memory, and what concepts fall under taxon memory? Refer to the chart on p. 50. How do you teach for each memory type? Are you teaching these concepts in the most effective way based on which type of memory that is needed?

Chapter 3

Teaching by Reaching All Students

1. Read the quotes from Part II and Chapter 3. Do you agree with this quote? Why or why not?

> *"Every student can learn, just not on the same day or in the same way."*
> — George Evans

_____
_____
_____
_____

2. What thoughts do you have as you read the lyrics from Tupac's song?

> *"The promise of a better tomorrow ain't never reached me, plus my teachers were too petrified in class to teach me."*
> — "Never B Peace", Tupac Shakur

9. What are some specific ways that we can build the English language while valuing the Spanish (or other native) language?

10. After reading the section on Long-Term English Learners (LTELs), how do we prevent LTELs? How do we move LTELs into academic and linguistic success? What does this look like in your classroom?

11. Go through each of the parts of VOICE. How do you (or can you) incorporate each of these into your classroom? Give specific examples. See VOICE Chart below.

12. What behaviors of learned helplessness have you seen in your class? What specific ways can you help move a student struggling with learned helplessness into academic success?

EL Saber Enterprises is a terrific resource for strategies for English Learners. See the chart below for specific strategies and activities. You can find information at www.elsaberenterprises.com.

Voice	Description	Strategies	
V	Visuals	• Pictures • Realia • Videos	• Anchor charts • Word walls • Posted directions
O	Oracy: "the ability to express oneself fluently and grammatically correct" (www.dictionary.com) academic dialogue, speaking about specific content	• Inside-outside circle • Think-pair-share-write • Turn and talk	• Question stems / response frames • Cooperative learning
I	Interactive Vocabulary: specifically and intentionally facilitating students to interact with vocabulary terms through conversation, games, and manipulation of words and meanings	• Interactive word wall games: musical words, unfolding 5 words in a story, draw me	• Concept definition maps • Open or Closed Word Sorts
C	Comprehension: understanding new information (orally or through text) in a given content area	• Survey Technique • Picture It	
E	Evaluation of Language	• Goal setting with students	• Rubrics based on TELPAS

3. What are your thoughts of structural racism? Have you ever experienced or seen how children have had inequity in their education based on structural racism?

4. Explore Hammond's quote on structural racism. How do we fight against the "apartheid" that seems to be unintentionally created in our school system?

> *Over time, because of structural racialization in education, we have seen a new type of intellectual apartheid happening in schools, creating dependent learners who cannot access the curriculum and independent learners who have had the opportunity to build the cognitive skills to do the deep learning on their own. Rather than stepping back, looking at the ways we structure inequity in education, and interrupting these practices, we simply focus on creating short-term solutions to get dependent students of color to score high on each year's standardized tests. We don't focus on building their intellective capacity so that they can begin to fill their own learning gaps with proper scaffolding. (31)*

5. Racial amnesia is a very important, yet controversial topic to discuss. How can we facilitate these needed conversations within our school buildings, even among our peers and friends, in a respectful, positive manner?

_____
_____
_____
_____
_____
_____
_____
_____
_____
_____

6. Have you seen the "cool pose" in action? What is your initial reaction to this posture? How does understanding this behavior help you with your reactions?

_____
_____
_____
_____
_____
_____
_____

7. Are there any microaggressions that you've heard on your campus or with your peers? What message do these phrases send to the students or others?

8. How do you value the Spanish language? If you hear it being spoken in a public place, or if you have to Press 1* on a recording to get to English, how do you *feel*? It's important to understand our own cultural bias (if there is one).

Chapter 4

Facing and *Moving Past* the Unique Challenges of Students of Poverty

1. Read the quote from Chapter 4. Do you agree with this quote? Is it sometimes difficult to have this perspective? Why or why not?

"Almost every student you meet might be fighting a battle you know nothing about. Stop. Think. Then make your response accordingly." (1)
— Author Unknown

_____
_____
_____
_____
_____
_____
_____
_____
_____
_____

2. What are some of the struggles you see parents in generational poverty struggling with, and how do you view these parents? With empathy? Judgment? Confusion?

3. How does chronic stress affect people (adults and children) living in generational poverty? Have you seen this in your own classrooms?

4. See the *Chart of Hardwired and Learned Traits* on p. 98. How do you see the learned traits at work in your own life? Have these become natural responses in your own life? How did you learn these?

_____
_____
_____
_____
_____
_____
_____
_____
_____
_____
_____
_____

5. How do we recognize when students have been taught traits outside of the 6 hardwired traits? How do we recognize when those students are choosing not to use these skills? How do we recognize when students have not been taught the learned traits? How do we teach those who need the learned traits?

_____
_____
_____
_____
_____
_____
_____

6. Discuss each of the scenarios on pages 98–102. How might you respond? Are there other scenarios that you see in your classroom? How can you teach your students the learned traits?

7. How can we help our students reduce their stress in our classroom environment to be able to open them up to education? Why can this not be overlooked?

Part III and Chapter 5

The Power of an Alliance

1. Take the time to read each of these lines in the following quote. Discuss your thoughts. What jumps out at you? What inspires you?

   "I've come to a frightening conclusion that I am the decisive element in the classroom. It's my personal approach that creates the climate. It's my daily mood that makes the weather. As a teacher, I possess a tremendous power to make a child's life miserable or joyous. I can be a tool of torture or an instrument of inspiration. I can humiliate or heal. In all situations, it is my response that decides whether a crisis will be escalated or de-escalated and a child humanized or dehumanized."

   — Haim Ginott

_____
_____
_____
_____
_____

2. Without calling out names, are there teachers on your campus that just don't seem to like students? How do their classrooms run? How do students perceive you?

> "Students work hardest for teachers they like and respect. When I'm asked, 'How do I get the students to like and respect me?' My immediate response is, 'Like and respect them first.'"
> — **Dr. Debbie Silver**

_____
_____
_____
_____
_____
_____
_____
_____
_____

3. What is the difference between an alliance and a relationship? Which are you intentionally building with your students? How?

_____
_____
_____
_____
_____
_____
_____
_____

4. What are some statements that you use consistently in your classroom when giving directions or redirecting? Do these statements lead to an alliance or a common goal?

5. Equity in relationships is so important and can be seen in *Response opportunities*, *Feedback*, and *Personal regard*. Read through the points under each strand. Discuss each point. What do you naturally do with your students? In what areas could you be more intentional? Give specific examples.

6. If we are not intentional about equitable relationships, what message might we send to students? If we ensure equity in relationships, what message are we sending? How does this message lead to learning?

_____
_____
_____
_____
_____
_____
_____
_____
_____
_____

7. After reading the blog *4 Steps to Influence the Underperformer – and Start the Move Past Learned Helplessness,* how do these steps look with your students? What is difficult about implementing these steps? How does having an authentic relationship make academic success more possible?

_____
_____
_____
_____
_____
_____
_____
_____
_____
_____

8. How do we counteract the "teacher vs. student" mentality?

Chapter 6

The Beauty of a Culturally Rich Environment

"Brains are designed to reflect the environments they're in, not rise above them. If we want our students to change, we must change ourselves and the environments students spend time in every day." [1]

— Eric Jenson

1. What is the environment in your class?

_____
_____
_____
_____
_____
_____
_____
_____

2. What are some of the times in your instruction when students seem to consistently struggle? Could a process or procedure be put into place or implemented with more fidelity?

_____
_____
_____
_____
_____
_____
_____
_____
_____
_____
_____
_____

3. How would you feel if you had an administrator with "moving expectations"? For example, sometimes lesson plans had to be done a certain way, sometimes it didn't matter, and other times, she wanted them to include other information! How do our students feel if they are trying to hit a moving target?

_____
_____
_____
_____
_____
_____
_____
_____
_____

4. What are some of the examples of behaviors or expectations that may be different because of culture?

5. Is your class more teacher-centered or student-centered? Give specific examples. Are there ways you could make it more student-centered?

6. What are some of the common struggles you find with cooperative learning? Which of these ideas could help with the implementation?

   a. Set, model and teach clear processes, procedures and expectations.
   b. Set the goals for learning, not completion.
   c. Plan the logistics based on the task and your students.
   d. Affirm voice and thought.

7. How do you use sentence frames currently? If you don't use sentence frames, how could these help your students?

8. How have you seen Johnson and Johnson's 5 Principles, found on p. 159, work? Which ones could you be a little more intentional implementing? How will you do that?

Strategies for Classroom Implementation

BUILDING INTERDEPENDENT LEARNING

- **Cube It**: Students are put into groups of six and numbered one through six. They are given a piece of paper folded into six squares. Someone in the group roles a dice. Whatever number it lands on is the number of the student who will be the scribe for that question. The teacher posts a question on the board. Everyone in the group writes their answer independently on that square. Then the group goes around the table and shares their answers. The scribe records all of the answers in that numbered box. For example, if the group roles a three, then the student who is number three records everyone's answers in box three, but everyone will have their own answers written in box number three of their individual papers. This strategy builds language and content in a safe environment. Teachers can vary the questions from Level 1 content area questions, to higher level opinion and metacognition questions. (Adapted from *Productive Group Work*)

- **Think-Pair-Share-Squared**: Students are paired high-low, and then pairs are paired up, so that in a group of four, you should have all levels of ability. Teacher posts a question, and students have intentional "think" time first. Then students pair up and share their thoughts with their partner. Because of the mixed grouping, I highly recommend using sentence frames here to guide the conversation and build the language. After the designated time for them to discuss, the partners then pair up to be a group of four and discuss. Again, I would start with sentence frames to facilitate conversation and provide language. (*Kagan Cooperative Learning* [Scaffolds added])

- **Dictogloss**: Students listen to the title of a text being read and make a prediction independently. Then they listen as the text is being read. Teacher will read through the text again as students take notes on important facts. Teacher reads through the text a third time as students fill in any gaps in any information. Then, as a cooperative group, students will rewrite the text word for word using their notes. Scaffolds can include a word bank and sentence starters. This task builds the listening domain of language, increases comprehension, and helps students work cooperatively. (*Stra-tiques*, EL Saber Enterprises)

Chapter 7

The Effectiveness of Hitting the Learning Target

"If a child can't learn the way we teach, maybe we should teach the way they learn."
— Ignacio Estrada

1. Do you agree with this quote? Why is this sometimes difficult?

_____
_____
_____
_____
_____
_____
_____
_____
_____

2. What does it mean on p. 170 when it says "*learning* definitely takes precedence over *doing*" in culturally responsive teaching? What could being focused on the *doing* look like? How do we move this into more *learning* focused instruction?

_____
_____
_____
_____
_____
_____
_____
_____
_____

3. Clarity asks these basic questions:

   a. What are you learning?
   b. Why are you learning it?
   c. How will you know when you learned it?

Why do you think teacher and student clarity is so important? Why do you think this can be overlooked sometimes?

_____
_____
_____
_____
_____
_____
_____
_____

4. How does ongoing feedback and formative assessment close achievement gaps? What does this look like in your content area?

5. How do we determine if task is meaningful? What are examples of tasks in your classroom that you have found meaningful? How do you know they were meaningful? Are there tasks that the students did not find meaningful? How do you know?

6. When is it appropriate to take a grade in your class? What are some common difficulties with grades?

7. Think about what you are teaching right now. Discuss how you can differentiate the context, process, and product for the particular lesson. Refer to pages 179–180 for ideas.

8. What struggles or deficits in vocabulary do you see with some of your students? Why do you think these exist? How can we counteract these deficits?

Strategies for Classroom Implementation

BUILDING VOCABULARY

- **Word Wall**: This strategy simply gets the words that are currently being learned up on the wall in a clear manner.

- **Musical Words**: Musical Words is a strategy that combines music, movement, and vocabulary! In this strategy, the teacher will break the students in groups of no more than five and have the students sit in a circle. Each student will be numbered (1, 2, 3, 4, 5). Each student chooses a word off of the word wall and writes it on a post-it note (make sure that each student in the group has the same size and color of post it notes) and turns it face down. When the music starts, students pass their words (still face down) to the right. When the music stops, the teacher calls out a number, and that numbered student holds the word they have up to their forehead without looking at it. The rest of the group gives clues to the student so that the student can guess their word. Once they guess it, the next number will hold their word up, and this will continue going until the teacher begins playing the music again. I would suggest doing 3–4 rounds. (EL Saber, 2015)

- **Draw Me**: Students will be paired with a partner. They need one piece of paper and one pencil between them. Partner A will start as the illustrator, and Partner B will be the guesser. Partner A begins drawing a word on the word wall as Partner B tries to guess the word. As soon as Partner B guesses the word, Partner A chooses another word and begins illustrating. Partner A is the illustrator for a minute. When the timer goes off, the partners switch, and Partner B becomes the illustrator and Partner A becomes the guesser. (EL Saber, 2015)

- **Concept Definition Map**: In a concept definition map, the idea is that students make personal connections to prior knowledge and experience, as they go deeper with a new concept. They may answer sentence frames like, "This reminds me of…" "An example is…" "A non-example is…" "An illustration is…" "An analogy is…" Typically this is done in a graphic organizer, such as a web. (EL Saber, 2015)

Appendix

The following surveys and chart are meant to be reproduced for training and planning. Thank you for using these tools to meet the needs and growth of all students!

Cultural Survey

1. How did your family identify ethnically or racially?

2. Where did you live-urban, suburban or rural community?

3. What is the story of your family in America? Has your family been here for generations or a few years?

4. How would you describe your family's economic status—middle class, upper class, working class, or low income? What did that mean in terms of quality of life?

5. Were you the first in your family to attend college? If not, who did?

6. What stories did you hear growing up?

7. List some family traditions—holidays, food, rituals.

8. Who were heroes celebrated in your family? Who were the "antiheroes?"

9. What were some "sayings" that you heard throughout your family growing up? What did they mean?

10. What did respect look like? Disrespect?

11. How were you trained to respond to different emotional displays—crying, anger, and happiness?

12. What physical, social, or cultural attributes were praised in your community? Which were you taught to avoid?

13. How were you expected to interact with authority figures? Was authority of teachers and other elders assumed or did it have to be earned?

14. As a child, did you call adults by their first name?

15. What got you shunned or shamed in your family? What earned you praise?

16. Were you allowed to question adults?

17. What's your family/community's relationship with time?

18. How were you expected to perform in school?

19. Were you given tangible rewards to performing in school, doing chores, etc, or were you expected to take care of responsibility?

20. In your classroom (life), what behavior do you expect your students or children to exhibit?

21. What were you taught about how other racial or ethnic groups succeeded or not?

22. Did you grow up thinking that people were born with intelligence?

23. Did you grow up believing that some groups are smarter than others?

24. How important is religion in your life, and do you believe it should be the foundation for others lives?

Cultural Survey — Students

1. How does your family identify ethnically or racially?

2. Where do you live-urban, suburban or rural community?

3. What is the story of your family in America? Has your family been here for generations or a few years?

4. Is college a goal of yours? Would you be the first person in your family to go to college? If not, who went to college?

5. List some family traditions—holidays, food, rituals.

6. Who are heroes celebrated in your family? Who are the "antiheroes?"

7. What does respect look like? Disrespect?

8. What is the appropriate way to respond to different emotional displays—crying, anger, and happiness—in your family?

9. How are you expected to interact with authority figures? Is authority of teachers and other elders assumed or does it have to be earned?

10. Were you allowed to question adults?

11. What's your family/community's relationship with time?

12. How are you expected to perform in school?

13. Are you given tangible rewards to performing in school, doing chores, etc., or were you expected to take care of responsibility?

14. What were you taught about reasons other racial or ethnic groups succeeded or not?

15. Do you think that people are born with intelligence?

16. How important is religion in your life, and do you believe it should be the foundation for others' lives?

BUILDING A BRIDGE 53

VOICE CHART

Voice	Description	Strategies
V	Visuals	- Pictures - Realia - Videos - Anchor charts - Word walls - Posted directions
O	Oracy: "the ability to express oneself fluently and grammatically correct" (www.dictionary.com) academic dialogue, speaking about specific content	- Inside-outside circle - Think-pair-share-write - Turn and talk - Question stems / response frames - Cooperative learning
I	Interactive Vocabulary: specifically and intentionally facilitating students to interact with vocabulary terms through conversation, games, and manipulation of words and meanings	- Interactive word wall games: musical words, unfolding 5 words in a story, draw me - Concept definition maps - Open or Closed Word Sorts
C	Comprehension: understanding new information (orally or through text) in a given content area	- Survey Technique - Picture It
E	Evaluation of Language	- Goal setting with students - Rubrics based on TELPAS

*Used with permission from EL Saber Enterprises

Culturally Responsive Teaching Checklist

In the planning:

☐   1. Start with the standard.

☐   2. What do the students have to **know**? What do the students have to **do**?

☐   3. Determine the vocabulary and teach explicitly.

☐   4. Create questions that are at the level of thinking required of the students to master the standard.

☐   5. Create activities that answer the question: "Does this activity lead my students to master the standard?"

☐   6. Scaffold for strugglers:
             a) Pre-teach vocabulary.
             b) Model the thinking.
             c) Build up the level of questions (start with level 1 and work up).
             d) Chunk the reading (*but require student reading*).
             e) Use sentence frames for conversation and/or writing.

☐   7. Provide a formative assessment with immediate feedback.

In the classroom:

☐   1. Make sure vocabulary is visual.

☐   2. Post directions and procedures.

☐   3. Post learning goal for the day and refer to it.

☐   4. Create and implement a way for students to get help (apart from you and always a neighbor).

- [ ] 5. Consider the gradual release model: You Do (You model), We Do (you and the students think together), We Do Together (cooperative learning where they think together), and I Do (individual work).

- [ ] 6. Facilitate academic interaction—they need to discuss the learning!

- [ ] 7. Provide anchor charts, graphic organizers, or notes for students to refer to when doing cooperative learning and individual work.

- [ ] 8. Provide *wait time* for processing and language.

- [ ] 9. Consider the collectivist vs. individualistic cultures—are grades the end goal? (This won't motivate many of your students.)

- [ ] 10. Provide structures and processes for the higher structure classes.

In the alliance:

- [ ] 1. Does every student know you care?

- [ ] 2. Do you have a particular way you greet each student?

- [ ] 3. Have you made positive contact with their parents or guardians?

- [ ] 4. Do you understand the collectivist mindset?
    a) Friends and family come first.
    b) Education may not be top priority.
    c) Relationships come before learning.

- [ ] 5. Do you have common goals?

Made in the USA
Monee, IL
02 May 2023